Let's Explore
Gravity

by Walt K. Moon

BUMBA BOOKS™

LERNER PUBLICATIONS ◆ MINNEAPOLIS

Note to Educators:

Throughout this book, you'll find critical thinking questions. These can be used to engage young readers in thinking critically about the topic and in using the text and photos to do so.

Lerner Publications Company
A division of Lerner Publishing Group, Inc.
241 First Avenue North
Minneapolis, MN 55401 USA

For reading levels and more information, look up this title at www.lernerbooks.com.

Library of Congress Cataloging-in-Publication Data

The Cataloging-in-Publication Data for *Let's Explore Gravity* is on file at the Library of Congress.
ISBN 978-1-5124-8269-0 (lib. bdg.)
ISBN 978-1-5415-1082-1 (pbk.)
ISBN 978-1-5124-8273-7 (EB pdf)

Manufactured in the United States of America
1 – CG – 12/31/17

Expand learning beyond the printed book. Download free, complementary educational resources for this book from our website, www.lerneresource.com.

Table of Contents

What Is Gravity?

Gravity is a force.

It is what pulls you toward the ground.

Earth has gravity.

It pulls objects toward its center.

Gravity makes a ball fall.

It makes a pencil drop to the floor.

Can you name any objects that float and don't fall to the ground?

You come back down when you jump.

Gravity pulls you to the floor.

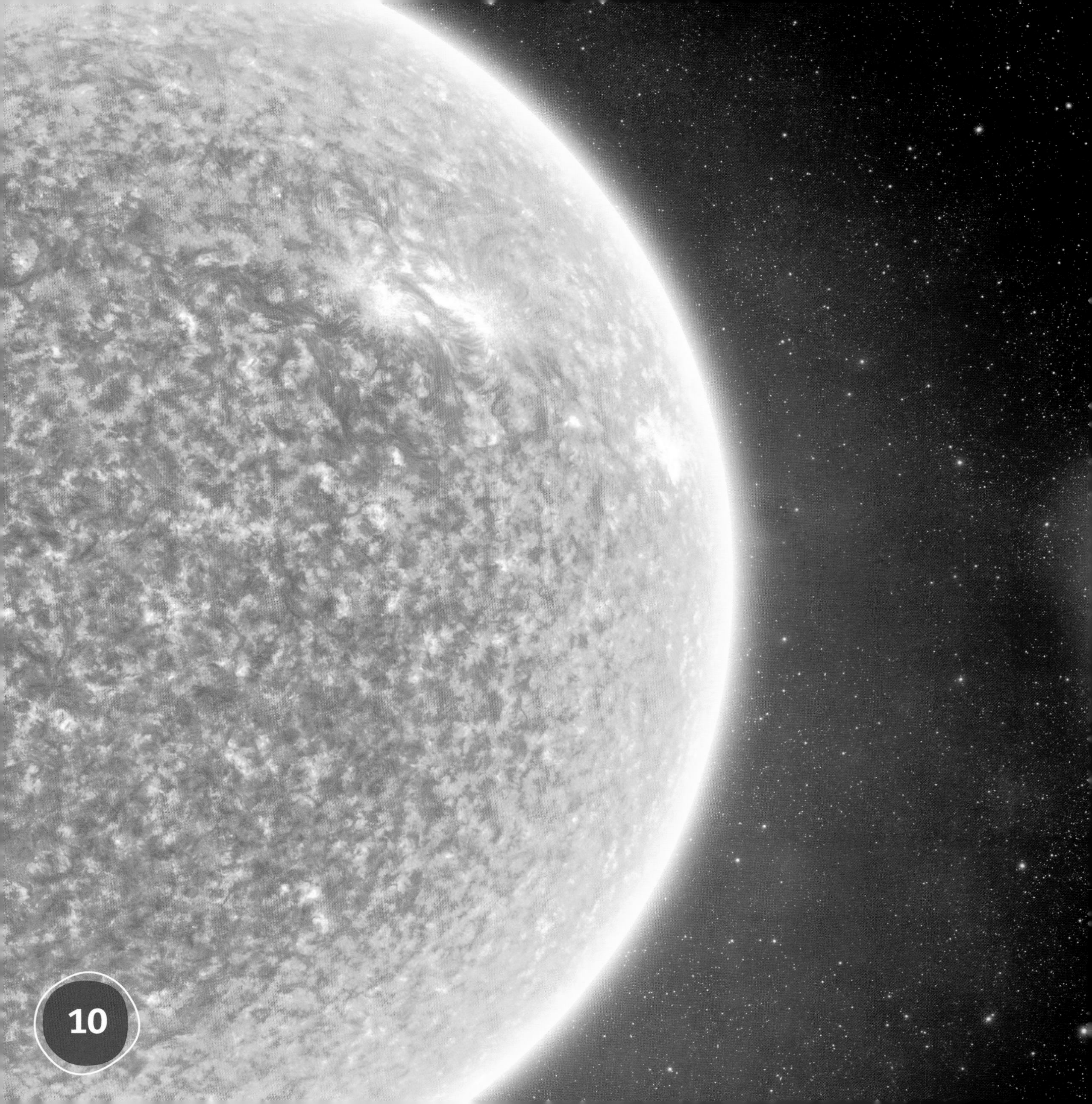

All objects have gravity.
Larger objects have
stronger gravity.
Smaller objects have
weaker gravity.
Gravity keeps Earth moving
around the sun.

The moon is smaller than Earth.

The moon has less gravity.

People weigh less on the moon.

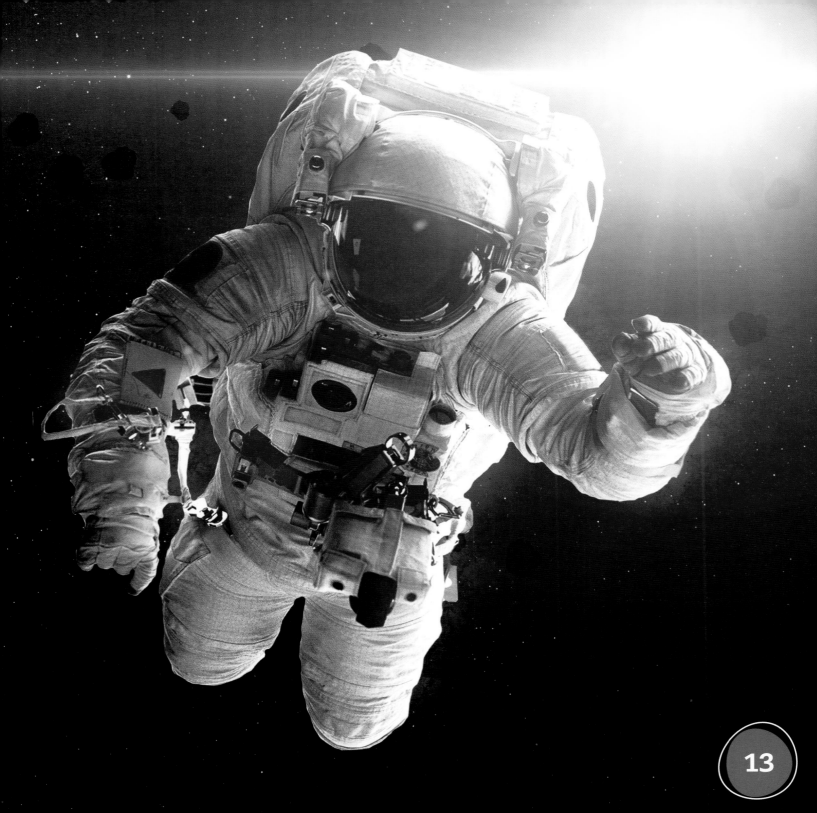

Birds fly.

They flap their wings to beat gravity.

Air holds them in the sky.

Can you name other animals or objects that fly in the air?

Our bodies work

against gravity.

Bones and muscles help us

stand and walk.

They push against gravity.

Try holding your arm out straight.

It might be easy at first.

But gravity eventually pulls your

arm down.

Gravity is strong.

How do you feel gravity?

Picture Quiz

Which of these pictures show something falling due to gravity?

Picture Glossary

force

a push or a pull, such as gravity, which pulls objects down

muscles

tissues in the body that help us move

pulls

moves something toward you

push

to move something by pressing

23

Read More

Chin, Jason. *Gravity.* New York: Roaring Brook Press, 2014.

Manolis, Kay. *Gravity.* Minneapolis: Bellwether Media, 2009.

Mayer, Lynne. *Newton and Me.* Mt. Pleasant, SC: Arbordale Publishing, 2013.

Index

Photo Credits